Gateways to Psychology
Visual Guides and Technology Tools

Dennis Coon

A. D. VanDeventer
Thomas Nelson Community College

THOMSON
WADSWORTH

Australia • Canada • Mexico • Singapore • Spain
United Kingdom • United States

Publisher: Edith Beard Brady
Senior Psychology Editor: Marianne Taflinger
Development Editor: Kristin Milotich
Assistant Editor: Jennifer Klos
Editorial Assistant: Kari Hopperstead
Technology Project Manager: Michelle Vardeman

Marketing Manager: Chris Caldeira
Production Service: Suzanne Kastner, Graphic World
  Publishing Services
Cover Image: Gary Cralle/Getty Images
Compositor: Graphic World Inc.
Printer: Quebecor World/Versailles

Printed in the United States of America
1 2 3 4 5 6 7 07 06 05 04 03

For more information about our products, contact us at:
Thomson Learning Academic Resource Center
1-800-423-0563
For permission to use material from this text, contact us by:
Phone: 1-800-730-2214
Fax: 1-800-730-2215
Web: http://www.thomsonrights.com

ISBN 0-534-61465-5

Wadsworth/Thomson Learning
10 Davis Drive
Belmont, CA 94002-3098
USA

Asia
Thomson Learning
5 Shenton Way #01-01
UIC Building
Singapore 068808

Australia/New Zealand
Thomson Learning
102 Dodds Street
Southbank, Victoria 3006
Australia

Canada
Nelson
1120 Birchmount Road
Toronto, Ontario M1K 5G4
Canada

Europe/Middle East/Africa
Thomson Learning
High Holborn House
50/51 Bedford Row
London WC1R 4LR
United Kingdom

Latin America
Thomson Learning
Seneca, 53
Colonia Polanco
11560 Mexico D.F.
Mexico

Spain/Portugal
Paraninfo
Calle/Magallanes, 25
28015 Madrid, Spain

Contents

This booklet is a study tool designed to help you better understand essential chapter concepts. For each chapter, this booklet provides a visual guide of key topics, Web sites to check out, links to related articles in InfoTrac College Edition's online library, and links to content on the *PsychNow! 2.0* and *Psyk.trek 2.0* CD-ROMs (your instructor may choose to assign either of these tutorial programs for your course.)

Visual Guides

Research has shown that, for some learners, presenting information in a visual format improves retention of material. The visual guides began several years ago with an individual instructor's attempt to give students a study tool in an alternative format that allowed them to review information as they prepared for examinations. You will read about the concept of cognitive mapping in Chapter 8, Conditioning and Learning, and about how educational psychologists attempt to improve the quality of learning in Chapter 20, Applied Psychology. Many of you will find the visual guides extremely helpful from the very beginning of your course. For others, you may discover their value as you proceed with your studies.

How do you make use of these visual guides? The Introduction to the main text discusses how to study psychology and explains the SQ4R method (a quick synopsis is also provided here). These visual guides are an integral part of the "S" ("Survey") and two of the "R's" ("Relate" and "Review").

Survey

Even before you survey the chapter, survey the visual guides. A preview like this gives you an overview of what material will be covered and highlights some key concepts that you will want to focus on.

Relate

The visual presentation demonstrates how one key topic relates to another. You may be surprised to see how many concepts are interconnected, and the visual guides provide an overview of these connections. Your long-term retention of the material can be improved by having an understanding of how the material you are studying relates to other material. The material in the visual guides is generally laid out in a top-down, left-to-right format. However, as you will see, the fact that most concepts are interrelated makes the exact layout of no great consequence.

Review

After you have read the chapter and want to test your mastery of the material, use the visual guides for review. At each point along the way, ask yourself:

- How much do I now know about each topic discussed here?
- What information do I now know that was not included in the visual guide?
- What items would I have added if I had been the creator of the visual guide?
- What questions is my instructor likely to ask about the topics that have been presented?

Some students may find it helpful to make detailed notes directly on the visual guides as they progress through the chapters.

Technology Tools

In addition to the visual guides of key concepts, links to a variety of technology tools are provided to give you an additional source of information on chapter topics. These tools include links to interesting Web sites, a list of related articles in InfoTrac College Edition, and links to related information on two interactive CD-ROMs: *PsychNow! 2.0* and *Psyk.trek 2.0*. These technology tools will help you learn more about the topics and will give you a head start in tracking down related information for research assignments and class projects. All URLs can be found on your text's companion Web site: *www.psychology.wadsworth. com/coon_gateways10e.*

We hope that you find these visual guides and links to related technology products a valuable study tool in mastering your course material.

PSYCHOLOGY

Psychology is the scientific study of behavior and mental processes. The professionals who create and apply psychological knowledge are called psychologists.

Ethical Standards

High ethical standards are an essential element of research in psychology.

Goals of Psychology

Psychologists gather information (data) in order to accomplish one or more of the four goals of psychology:

1. Describe: to organize information for further research
2. Understand: to know what prompts behaviors
3. Predict: to be able to anticipate the consequences of events
4. Control: to improve the human condition

Scientific Method

To conduct their research, psychologists use the scientific method, which is a very powerful way to observe the natural world and to form valid conclusions about human behavior.

Critical Thinking

Critical thinking is central to applying the scientific method, to psychology as a scientific field, and to effective behavior in general.

Media

The media (TV, magazines, movies, and newspapers) are full of inaccurate information. All information, from whatever source, should be evaluated critically.

1. Observe Behaviors

Psychologists are observers. Events in the natural world prompt them to want to understand relationships in behavior. Observations prompt asking questions and seeking answers.

2. Define the Problem

When conducting research, the observations must be organized in a logical manner.

3. Propose a Hypothesis

- Based on what has been observed thus far, the psychologist creates a tentative ("educated guess") explanation of an event or relationship.
- A hypothesis must be testable.

4. Conduct Research

- Research is done to collect information in an organized, scientific manner.
- Gather evidence and test the hypothesis.
- Research may be done in a variety of ways:

5. Publish Results

Research results prompt discussion and debate. New theories are formed, and new areas of research are suggested.

6. Formulate Theory

A theory summarizes the existing data and predicts future observations. The process begins again using the new data.

Naturalistic Observation

Studies the behaviors of human and animals in natural settings.

Correlational Method

Takes measurements to discover the relationship between two events that appear to be connected.

Clinical Method

Reviews accidents or natural events that have affected an individual (or groups of individuals).

Survey Method

Asks questions about human behavior, thoughts, and attitudes.

Experimental Method

Designs a structured, controlled environment. The controls established by the formal experimental method are the best method for determining cause-and-effect relationships in psychology.

CHAPTER

1

Introduction to Psychology and Research Methods

Psychology on the Web

To link to the following sites, visit *www.psychology.wadsworth.com/coon_gateways10e*

American Psychological Association
Home page of the APA, with links to PsychNET, student information, member information, and more.

American Psychological Society
Home page of the APS, with links to information, services, and Internet resources.

Ethical Principles of Psychologists and Code of Conduct
The full text of the ethical principles that guide professional psychologists.

Psychweb
This award-winning page provides a multitude of services and links.

Psycoloquy
An online journal with short articles on all areas of psychology.

PsycPORT
This site is a large database of psychological information, including daily updates on news related to psychology.

Today in the History of Psychology
Events in the history of psychology by the date.

Related Articles in InfoTrac College Edition

Go to *http://www.infotrac-college.com/wadsworth* and search by article number.

A87022736
Adams, J. (2002, March–April). Keep a diary, reap cognitive rewards. *Psychology Today, 35*(2), 28(1). Mag.Coll.: 111H1103.

A79981551
Benson, N. (2000, November). The humanistic perspective. *Psychology Review, 7*(2), 32.

A79381589
Benson, N. (2000, April). Behaviorism (part 3). *Psychology Review, 6*(4), 32.

A96736801
Konrad, A., & Harris, C. (2002, September). Desirability of the Bem Sex-Role Inventory items for women and men: A comparison between African Americans and European Americans (1). *Sex Roles: A Journal of Research*, p. 259(13).

A91475110
Sprecher, S., & Toro-Morn, M. (2002, March). A study of men and women from different sides of earth to determine if men are from Mars and women are from Venus in their beliefs about love and romantic relationships (1). (Statistical data included). *Sex Roles: A Journal of Research*, p. 131(17).

A97310595
Feds to begin clinical tests on drugs commonly prescribed for children. (2003, February 16). *Medical Letter on the CDC & FDA*, p. 20.

A97309842
Praxis Pharmaceuticals updates shareholders on financing and clinical trials. (2003, February 12). *Biotech Week*, p. 96.

Interactive Learning

Links to the *PsychNow!* and *Psyk.trek* CD-ROMs:

PsychNow! 2.0 1b. Psychology and Its History, 1c. Research Methods, 1d. Critical Thinking in Psychology.

Psyk.trek 2.0 1. History and Methods.

BIOPSYCHOLOGY

Psychologists who study how processes in the body, brain, and nervous system relate to behavior are called biopsychologists.

Nerve Cell Activity

Ultimately, nerve cell activity is the source of all experience and behavior.

Central Nervous System

The brain and the spinal column form the central nervous system (CNS).

Peripheral Nervous System

All the parts of the nervous system outside the brain and the spinal cord form the peripheral nervous system (PNS).

Endocrine System

Endocrine glands serve as a chemical communications system within the body. Behavior is greatly influenced by the ebb and flow of hormones in the bloodstream.

The Brain

The brain is the largest center of nerve cell activity. Brain activities and structures are associated with all human capacities.

Human Experiences

All sensations, thoughts, feelings, motives, actions (behaviors), and memories stem from brain activity.

Recordings and Images

Bioelectrical recordings and computer-generated images of brain activity provide additional insight into how the brain works. Brain dominance and brain activity determine whether you are right-handed, left-handed, or ambidextrous.

Brain Mapping

To determine how the brain works, biopsychologists attempt to determine which areas of the brain are responsible for specific behaviors by mapping the brain. Brain mapping is done by activating or disabling specific areas of the brain and observing whether behaviors cease, continue, or change.

Neurogenesis

The brain's circuitry is not static. The brain grows new nerve cells and can "rewire" itself in response to changing environmental conditions.

Psychology on the Web

To link to the following sites, visit *www.psychology.wadsworth.com/ coon_gateways10e*

Brain Briefings
Articles on a variety of topics in neuroscience.

Brain Connection
Explains brain research to the public, including common myths about the brain, the effects of various chemicals, how brain research applies to education, and more.

Lorin's Left-handedness Site
Answers to common questions about left-handedness.

Probe the Brain
Explore the motor homunculus of the brain interactively.

The Brain Quiz
Answer questions about the brain and get instant feedback.

The Brain: A Work in Progress
A set of related articles about the brain.

The Human Brain: Dissections of the Real Brain
Detailed photographs and drawings of the human brain.

The Endocrine System
Describes the endocrine system and hormones.

Related Articles in InfoTrac College Edition

Go to *http://www.infotrac-college.com/wadsworth* and search by article number.

A54772954
Hiller-Sturmhofel, S., & Bartke, A. (1998, Summer). The endocrine system: An overview. *Alcohol Health & Research World, 22*(3), 153. Mag.Coll.: 98K2542.

A79894657
Link unearthed between lefties in family and memory. (2001, November 12). *Pain & Central Nervous System Week*, p. 22. (Brief article.)

A82261834
Budgar, L. (2001, November–December). Say again: Stuttering may be more than a case of nerves. *Psychology Today, 34*(6), 16. Mag.Coll.: 109J0691. (This study finds possible physiological cause of speech disorder. Brief article.)

A87781225
Spear, L. P. (2002, March). The adolescent brain and the college drinker: Biological basis of propensity to use and misuse alcohol. *Journal of Studies on Alcohol, 63*(2), S71(11).

A82033489
McLellan, F. (2002, January 19). Countering poverty's hindrance of neurodevelopment. *The Lancet, 359*(9302), 236. Mag.Coll.: 109F4425. (News. Brief article.)

Interactive Learning

Links to the *PsychNow!* and *Psyk.trek* CD-ROMs:

PsychNow! 2.0 3a. Neurons and Synaptic Transmission, 3b. Brain and Behavior.

Psyk.trek 2.0 2. Biological Bases of Behavior, Psyk.trek Simulations: 2. Hemispheric Specialization.

CHILD DEVELOPMENT

Psychologists who study human growth and development are known as <u>developmental psychologists</u>.

Nature vs. Nurture

Of particular interest in child development are the interactions of <u>nature versus nurture</u>.

Effect of Nature and Nurture

You are a product of your genetic heritage and the environments in which you have lived.

Nature *(Heredity)*

A person's genetic makeup influences his or her temperament, susceptibility to disease, potential cognitive abilities, and a great deal more.

Genetic Research

Genetic research is making it possible to control some hereditary aspects of human reproduction, development, and behavior.

Nurture *(Environment)*

Environmental factors such as parental involvement, socioeconomic situation, religion, personal experiences, and many others are important to the child.

Nutrition

Maintaining good nutrition during pregnancy is important to the fetus's development.

Deprivation and Enrichment

All areas of child development are affected by conditions of deprivation (lack of normal stimulation, comfort, love) or enrichment (a deliberately made complex, stimulating, supportive environment).

Parenting

Parents (caregivers) may be the single greatest influence in a child's environment.

Learning

Children come into the world with simple reflexes, but prepared to acquire knowledge.

Child Discipline

To be effective, child discipline should be:
- Consistent
- Humane
- Encouraging
- Based on respectful communication

Emotional Bonding

Forming an emotional bond with a caregiver is a crucial event during infancy.

Stage Theory

Piaget's theory of child development through stages provides a valuable map of how thinking (cognitive) abilities unfold.

Sociocultural Theory

Vygotsky's theory reminds us that a child's mind is shaped by human relationships.

Language

Learning language is a cornerstone of early intellectual development.

Psychology on the Web

To link to the following sites, visit *www.psychology.wadsworth.com/coon_gateways10e*

Choosing Quality Child Care
Provides information on issues related to quality child care.

Depression After Delivery
A site devoted to providing information about postpartum depression.

Diving into the Gene Pool
From the Exploratorium, teaches about modern genetics.

Human Relations Publications
Covers more than 50 topics spanning the entire range of human development.

I Am Your Child
Information for parents of children up to 3 years of age.

Jean Piaget Archives: Biography
The life of Jean Piaget, plus five photos from birth to old age.

Parenthood Web
A comprehensive site for parents.

Sesame Street Parents
An expert description of physical development from birth to 11.

The Parent's Page
Comprehensive site full of links for expectant couples and new parents.

Related Articles in InfoTrac College Edition

Go to *http://www.infotrac-college.com/wadsworth* and search by article number.

A92524864
Greenfield, S. (2002, September 21). Nature versus nurture: The state of play. *Spectator, 290*(9085), 42(2).

A93093428
Lemonick, M. (2002, October 28). What makes us do it? In the age-old debate of nature vs. nurture, an M.I.T. prof says our genes don't get enough respect. *Time, 160*(18), 54.

A96125478
Insecure attachment a risk factor for depression. (What's new in research). (2003, January). *The Brown University Child and Adolescent Behavior Letter, 19*(1), 5(2). (Brief article.)

A93305717
McClowry, S., & Galehouse, P. (2002, July–September). Planning a temperament-based parenting program for inner-city families. *Journal of Child and Adolescent Psychiatric Nursing, 15*(3), 97(9).

A72093183
Sandler, A. (2001, February). Attachment disorder behavior following early severe deprivation: Extension and longitudinal follow-up. *Journal of Developmental & Behavioral Pediatrics, 22*(1), 80.

Interactive Learning

Links to the *PsychNow!* and *Psyk.trek* CD-ROMs:

PsychNow! 2.0 2a. Infant Development, 2b. Child Development, 2c. Adolescent Development, 2d. Adult Development, Aging, and Death.

Psyk.trek 2.0 9. Human Development.

LIFE-SPAN DEVELOPMENT

Life-span psychologists identify general patterns that provide an approximate map of human development.

Continuity and Change

Development over a lifetime is marked by both continuity and changes in behavior.

Parenting

Many of us will become parents and play a key role in early life-span development of children.

Childhood Problems

Parents must be able to distinguish normal childhood problems from those that are more serious.

Child Abuse

The incidence of child abuse could be reduced with appropriate social and psychological efforts.

Personal Development

Personal development does not end after adolescence. Periods of stability and transition occur throughout adulthood.

Developmental Tasks

Erik Erikson analyzed a series of psychological challenges (psychosocial dilemmas) that occur across the life span. These range from gaining trust in infancy to living with integrity in old age.

Morality

Developing mature moral standards is also important during adolescence.

Aging

Physical aging starts early in adulthood. Every adult must find ways to successfully cope with aging.

The End of Life

Death is a natural part of life. There is value in understanding it and accepting it.

Trust
Learning to trust others and the world comes from good parental care.

Autonomy
Developing self-control and independence is essential to the developing sense of self and self-esteem.

Initiative
Learning to make plans and carry them out is necessary for living in the adult world.

Industry
Achieving goals and being recognized is important to our sense of self-esteem.

Identity
Forming a personal identity is a major task of adolescence.

Intimacy
Establishing a circle of friends, family, and a spouse/partner.

Generativity
Being productive and developing an interest in guiding the next generation.

Meaning and Integrity
Successful lives are based on happiness, purpose, meaning, and integrity.

CHAPTER

4 From Birth to Death: Life-Span Development

Psychology on the Web
To link to the following sites, visit *www.psychology.wadsworth.com/coon_gateways10e*

Alzheimer's Association
Has many links to material on Alzheimer's disease.

Mental Health Risk Factors for Adolescents
Links to resources concerning eating disorders, drug abuse, suicide, and other topics.

MIDMAC
Reports on a major study of middle age.

The AARP Webplace
Home page of the American Association of Retired Persons.

WWW Loss Resources
A list of links to sites on death, grief, and loss.

What Works for Girls
A summary of research about what contributes positively to healthy development.

Related Articles in InfoTrac College Edition
Go to *http://www.infotrac-college.com/wadsworth* and search by article number.

A71761785
Cross, T. (2001, Winter). Gifted children and Erikson's theory of psychosocial development. *Gifted Child Today*, 24(1), 54.

A76627696
Elkind, D. (2001). *The hurried child: Growing up too fast, too soon* (3rd ed., p. 288). Perseus.

A20615259
Meyers, S. (1998, June). Personality correlates of adult attachment style. *The Journal of Social Psychology*, 138(3), 407(3).

A96554697
Christopher and Peter Hitchens square off. (2003, January–February). *Book*, p. 14(1). (Brief article.)

A97484947
Bussing, R., Gary, F., Mason, D., Leon, C., Sinha, K., Garvan, C. W., & Wilson, C. (2003, February). Child temperament, ADHD, and caregiver strain: Exploring relationships in an epidemiological sample. *Journal of the American Academy of Child and Adolescent Psychiatry*, 42(2), 184(9).

A97484948
Connor, D., Edwards, G., Fletcher, K., Baird, J., Barkley, R., & Steingard, R. (2003, February). Correlates of comorbid psychopathology in children with ADHD. *Journal of the American Academy of Child and Adolescent Psychiatry*, 42(2), 193(8).

A98315280
Atlanta study says disorder more common than thought (autism). (2003, January 26). *Medical Letter on the CDC & FDA*, p. 11.

Interactive Learning
Links to the *PsychNow!* CD-ROM:

PsychNow! 2.0 2c. Adolescent Development, 2d. Adult Development, Aging, and Death.

SENSATION

The immediate response in the brain caused by excitation of a sensory organ.

Sensory Systems

Sensory systems select, analyze, and transduce information from the surrounding world and send it to the brain.

Synesthesia

- The existence of synesthesia suggests that the senses are not entirely isolated from one another.
- Our private sensory worlds are made up of a complex blend of information from all of the senses.

Relation to External Stimuli

Private sensations do not correspond perfectly to external stimuli. Studies in psychophysics relate physical energies to the sensations we experience.

Eyes

Loss of vision may be the single most devastating sensory disability.

Ears

Our hearing provides the brain with a wealth of information not available from other senses.

Nose

Our sense of smell contributes to our enjoyment of food.

Tongue

Our sense of taste adds variety and excitement to nutrition.

Skin

Our skin provides us with information about pressure (touch), temperature, and pain.

Other Senses

- Kinesthetic (monitors position of parts of the body)
- Vestibular (provides information about the body's position in space)

Process

- All of the senses rely on a complex series of <u>mechanical</u>, <u>chemical</u>, and <u>neural</u> events to convert stimuli into messages understood by the brain.
- Only a small part of the sensory information surrounding us actually reaches the brain or registers there. <u>Sensory adaptation</u>, <u>selective attention</u>, and <u>sensory gating</u> significantly modify our experiences.

Vision

The eyes and the brain form a complex system for sensing light. Vision is based on an active, computer-like analysis of light patterns.

Pain

Pain can be reduced or controlled by altering factors that affect pain intensity.

CHAPTER

5 Sensation and Reality

Psychology on the Web

To link to the following sites, visit *www.psychology.wadsworth.com/coon_gateways10e*

HEARNET
A page that promotes ear protection for rock musicians.

How We See
A tutorial on the basic processes of vision provided by Access Excellence at the National Health Museum.

Interactive Illustrations of Color Perception
Examples of how colors interact with each other. These interactive illusions were created for the color theory portion of a computer graphics course at Brown University.

Questions and Answers About Pain Control
Answers common questions about pain control.

Smell
Olfaction and problems with smelling are defined.

Smell and Taste Disorders FAQ
Questions and answers about smell and taste disorders.

Vestibular Disorders Association
Provides links to sites concerned with vestibular problems.

Related Articles in InfoTrac College Edition

Go to *http://www.infotrac-college.com/wadsworth* and search by article number.

A88243012
Scientists detail how brain regulates sensory information. (2002, July 8). *Pain & Central Nervous System Week*, p. 7.

A18158438
Emery, C. E., Jr. (1996, March–April). When the media miss real messages in subliminal stories. *Skeptical Inquirer, 20*(2), 16(3).

A96286106
New detection technique described. (for diagnosing diabetic retinopathy). (2003, January 13). *Diabetes Week*, p. 12.

A96519690
FDA clears SurgiLight to initiate trials of OptiVision laser reversal. (Food and Drug Administration) (SurgiLight Inc.). (2003, January 26). *Medical Devices & Surgical Technology Week*, p. 28.

A5038380
Chance, P. (1987, July). Blinding stress. (stress can cause detached retina). *Psychology Today, 21*, 22(2). Mag.Coll.: 40A1649.

A96267584
Boettcher, F. (2002, December). Presbyacusis and the auditory brainstem response. *Journal of Speech, Language, and Hearing Research, 45*(6), 1249(13).

A93722736
Fast-paced gene discovery changes clinical care of deaf patients. (2002, November 4). *Health & Medicine Week*, p. 2.

A84546027
When brains wring colors from words. (Behavior). (2002, March 23). *Science News, 161*(12), 189(1). Mag.Coll.: 110G0014. (Brief article.)

Interactive Learning

Links to the *PsychNow!* and *Psyk.trek* CD-ROMs:

PsychNow! 2.0 4a. Vision and Hearing, 4b. Chemical and Somesthetic Senses.

Psyk.trek 2.0 3a. Light and the Eye, 3b. Retina, 3c. Vision and the Brain, 3d. Perception of Color, 3h. The Sense of Hearing.

PERCEPTION

Perception is an <u>active process</u> of assembling <u>sensations</u> into meaningful patterns that represent external events.

Gestalt Principles

We unconsciously use Gestalt principles to organize sensations into meaningful patterns.

Constancies

Our vision would be unstable and would seem distorted and erratic if not for the perceptual constancies of:
- Size
- Shape
- Brightness

Vision

Our eyes make major contributions to our perceptual experience.

Perceptual Influences

Perception is greatly affected by factors such as:
- Learning
- Values
- Motives
- Expectations
- Attention

Private perceptual experiences do not always accurately represent external events.

EXTRASENSORY PERCEPTION (ESP)

Reported abilities to perceive events in ways that cannot be explained by known sensory capacities is known as extrasensory perception.

Evidence

Scientific evidence concerning the existence of extrasensory perception is mostly <u>negative</u> or <u>inconclusive</u>.

Abilities

The ability to perceive events or information in ways that are affected by distance (clairvoyance), the ability to read minds (telepathy), the ability to predict future events (precognition), and the ability to influence objects purely with the mind are all considered to be extrasensory.

3-D

The right and the left eye see different things. This difference is <u>retinal disparity</u> and gives us our wondrous ability to perceive three-dimensional space.

Depth Perception

<u>Bodily cues</u> and <u>pictorial cues</u> provide added information about depth and distance.

Perceptual Accuracy

The accuracy and objectivity of perceptions can be improved through conscious effort and an awareness of factors that contribute to erroneous perceptions.

Misperception

Eyewitnesses frequently misperceive events—even important events such as crimes or accidents.

Psychology on the Web

To link to the following sites, visit *www.psychology.wadsworth.com/coon_gateways10e*

IllusionWorks
A large collection of visual illusions.

Perceptual Processes
A collection of tutorials and demonstrations related to our senses.

Stereogram Links
Provides links to stereograms and information about stereograms, including how to create your own.

The Joy of Visual Perception
An online book about visual perception.

Vision Test
An on-screen vision test.

Visual Illusions Gallery
Presents 24 visual illusions for fun and exploring the nature of perception.

Related Articles in InfoTrac College Edition

Go to *http://www.infotrac-college.com/wadsworth* and search by article number.

A94510934
Bower, B. (2002, November 9). Visual structure grips infants' attention. *Science News, 162*(19), 293(2). Mag.Coll.: 112D0038.

A76769656
Evans, D., Elliott, J. M., & Packard, M. (2001, July). Visual organization and perceptual closure are related to compulsive-like behavior in typically developing children. (Statistical data included). *Merrill-Palmer Quarterly, 47*(3), 323.

A53560428
Gregory, R. (1998, December 19). Snapshots from the decade of the brain: Brainy mind. (Clinical review). *British Medical Journal, 317*(7174), 1693(3).

A98592228
Wagstaff, G. F., Macveigh, J., Boston, R., Scott, L., Brunas-Wagstaff, J., & Cole, J. (2003, January). Can laboratory findings on eyewitness testimony be generalized to the real world? An archival analysis of the influence of violence, weapon presence, and age on eyewitness accuracy. *The Journal of Psychology, 137*(1), 17(12).

A92203282
Thompson, S. (2002, July–August). Do dogs have ESP? *National Geographic World,* p. 6(1). (Research on dog's psychic abilities.)

A82066914
Radin, D. (2001, December). A dog that seems to know when his owner is coming home: Effect of environmental variables. *The Journal of Parapsychology, 65*(4), 374(1). (Abstract)

Interactive Learning

Links to the *PsychNow!* and *Psyk.trek* CD-ROMs:

PsychNow! 2.0 4c. Perception.

Psyk.trek 2.0 3e. Gestalt Psychology, 3f. Depth Perception, 3g. Visual Illusions.

Photo: © Adrian Weinbrecht/photolibrary/PictureQuest

CONSCIOUSNESS

To be conscious means to be aware. Consciousness consists of all the sensations, perceptions, memories, and feelings we are aware of at any instant.

Altered States

Consciousness and altered states of awareness are core features of mental life.
- Sleep is the most common form of an altered state of consciousness (ASC).
- Some chemicals may also produce ASCs.

Sleep

Sleep is necessary for survival of the individual. Mental illness or death may result from insufficient sleep.

REM and Non-REM Sleep

Sleep occurs in two basic states: rapid eye movement (REM) sleep and non-REM sleep.

Four Stages of Sleep

Sleep occurs in four stages, ranging from shallow to deep. Each stage is marked by different brain wave patterns.

Sleep Disorders

Sleep disorders (apnea, narcolepsy, and sleepwalking) and sleep loss are serious health problems that should be corrected if they persist.

Psychoactive Drugs

Psychoactive drugs (those that modify brain function) are highly prone to abuse because of their ability to alter consciousness.

Personal Maladjustment

Drug abuse is related to personal maladjustment, the reinforcing qualities of drugs, peer group influences, and expectations about drug effects.

Uppers

Drugs such as cocaine, caffeine, and nicotine excite the brain.

Downers

Drugs such as alcohol, tranquilizers, and sedatives inhibit brain function.

Hallucinogens

Marijuana and other hallucinogenic drugs may have a variety of effects on brain and body.

Hypnosis

Hypnosis is useful, but not "magical." Hypnosis can change private experiences more readily than behaviors or habits.

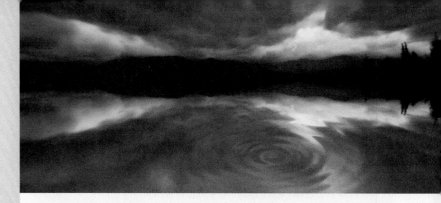

REM

REM sleep helps us form memories and contributes to general mental effectiveness. REM sleep is generally associated with dreaming. Non-REM sleep is generally free of dreams.

Dreams

Dreams are at least as meaningful as waking thoughts. Whether dreams have deeper, symbolic meaning is still debated. Collecting and interpreting your dreams can promote self-awareness.

CHAPTER

7 States of Consciousness

Psychology on the Web
To link to the following sites, visit *www.psychology.wadsworth.com/coon_gateways10e*

Alcoholics Anonymous (AA)
Home page of Alcoholics Anonymous.

Circadian Rhythms
Basic information about circadian rhythms and jet lag.

Cocaine Anonymous
Offers advice and information on how to overcome cocaine addiction.

Drugs and Behavior Links
Comprehensive links to topics in drugs and behavior.

Marijuana Anonymous
Offers advice and information on how to quit smoking marijuana.

Self-Scoring Alcohol Check-Up
A short quiz for identifying drinking problems.

SleepNet
Information about sleep and sleep disorders, with many links to other sites.

Sudden Infant Death and Other Infant Death
Information about SIDS, with links to related topics.

The Antidrug.com
Advice to parents and other adults about how to help children resist drug use.

Related Articles in InfoTrac College Edition
Go to *http://www.infotrac-college.com/wadsworth* and search by article number.

A86482527
Hypnosis: Theory and application part II. (2002, June). *Harvard Mental Health Letter, 18*(12).

A97177907
Perk up in the afternoon. (2003, March). *Natural Health, 33*(2), 40(2). (Ask the experts: Answers to your questions from the leaders in natural medicine.)

A98044306
Poor sleep linked to earlier death in older adults. (2003, February 24). *Health & Medicine Week,* p. 37.

A81873185
Bradbury, J. (2002, January 12). Common drugs and the pursuit of a good night's sleep. *The Lancet, 359*(9301), 140. Mag.Coll.: 109F4319.

A17782612
Gardner, M. (1995, November–December). Waking up from Freud's theory of dreams. (Notes of a fringe-watcher). *Skeptical Inquirer, 19*(6), 10(4).

Interactive Learning
Links to the *PsychNow!* and *Psyk.trek* CD-ROMs:

PsychNow! 2.0 3c. Sleep and Dreaming, 3d. Psychoactive Drugs.

Psyk.trek 2.0 4b. Sleep, 4c. Abused Drugs and Their Effects, 4d. Drugs and Synaptic Transmissions.

Photo: Donald C. Landwehrle/Getty Images

LEARNING

Learning is a <u>relatively permanent change</u> in behavior due to experience. *Temporary changes in behavior due to motivation, drugs, injury, or disease are not learning.*

Behavior Modification

• Learning principles can be used to manage one's own behavior or the behavior of others.
• To understand why people behave as they do, it is important to identify how their responses are being reinforced.

Conditioning

Conditioning is a fundamental type of learning that affects many aspects of daily life.

Cognitive Learning

Cognitive learning involves acquiring higher level information, rather than just linking stimuli and responses.

Observational Learning (Modeling)

We also learn by observing and imitating the actions of others.

BIOLOGY AND BEHAVIOR

Biological behavior patterns facilitate the learning of some responses while making others more difficult to learn.

Instincts

Some behaviors in animals are <u>instinctive</u> and may prevent learning some responses. Other responses may be easier to learn because of biological programming.

Classical Conditioning

In this form of learning, the responses are reflexive (involuntary).

- In classical conditioning, a <u>neutral stimulus (NS)</u> is one that does not cause a response. It is repeatedly paired with an unconditioned stimulus.
- An <u>unconditioned stimulus (US)</u> is a stimulus that reliably provokes a response (typically physiological and/or emotional). This involuntary response is an <u>unconditioned response (UR)</u>.
- By association, the neutral stimulus also begins to elicit a response. The neutral stimulus is no longer neutral. It has become a <u>conditioned stimulus (CS)</u>.

Operant Conditioning

In this form of learning, the <u>consequences</u> of behavior determine whether the behavior will be repeated (voluntary).

Reinforcement

Responses that are followed by <u>reinforcement</u> become more frequent.

Punishment

Responses that are followed by punishment (an aversive stimulus or removal of a positive event) become less frequent.

Psychology on the Web

To link to the following sites, visit *www.psychology.wadsworth.com/ coon_gateways10e*

Animal Training at Sea World
Explains how marine mammals are trained at Sea World.

Memory
A short tutorial on classical conditioning, operant conditioning, and cognitive learning.

Methods for Changing Behavior
Teaches you how to modify your own behavior.

Observational Learning
Presents Bandura's original work on modeling, with graphs.

Oppatoons
Cartoons of rats undergoing conditioning.

Studying Television Violence
An article on television violence.

Related Articles in InfoTrac College Edition

Go to *http://www.infotrac-college.com/wadsworth* and search by article number.

A13858761
Blackman, D., & Pellon, R. (1993, February). The contributions of B. F. Skinner to the interdisciplinary science of behavioural pharmacology. *British Journal of Psychology, 84*(1), 1(23).

A95447417
McSweeney, F., & Samantha, S. (2002, October). Common processes may contribute to extinction and habituation. *The Journal of General Psychology, 129*(4), 364(37).

A75705750
Heflin, J., & Alberto, A. (2001, Summer). Establishing a behavioral context for learning for students with autism. *Focus on Autism and Other Developmental Disabilities, 16*(2), 93.

A63789322
Hancock, D. (2000, July). Impact of verbal praise on college students' time spent on homework. (Statistical data included.) *The Journal of Educational Research, 93*(6), 384.

A82299589
Salemi, M. (2002, January). An illustrated case for active learning. (Targeting teaching.) *Southern Economic Journal, 68*(3), 721(11) Bus.Coll.: 138N0759.

A64075961
Reading, writing, and rote learning drive students to western schools. (2000, August 14). *Business Week*, (3694), 4.

Interactive Learning

Links to the *PsychNow!* and *Psyk.trek* CD-ROMs:

PsychNow! 2.0 5a. Classical Conditioning, 5b. Operant Conditioning, 5c. Observational Learning.

Psyk.trek 2.0 5a. Overview of Classical Conditioning, 5b. Basic Processes in Classical Conditioning, 5c. Overview of Operant Conditioning, 5d. Schedules of Reinforcement, 5e. Reinforcement and Punishment, 5f. Avoidance and Escape Learning.

MEMORY

Memory is an <u>active process</u> in which information is received, organized, altered, stored, and recovered. Memories are often lost, altered, revised, or distorted.

Sensory, Short-Term, and Long-Term Memory

Different strategies are required to make the best use of short-term memory and long-term memory.

Memory Limitations

Limitations of memory that sometimes appear to be flaws are actually adaptive and desirable in most circumstances. It is not necessarily beneficial for us to "remember" everything.

Recovered Memories

Extreme caution is warranted when "recovered" memories are the only basis for believing that a person was sexually abused during childhood.

Remembering

Remembering is not an all-or-nothing process. Information that appears to be lost may still reside in memory.

Improving Memory

Although it's true that some people have naturally superior memories, everyone can learn to improve his or her memory.

Memory Systems

Memory systems (mnemonics) greatly improve immediate memory. However, conventional learning tends to create the most lasting memories.

Retrieval Failure (Forgetting)

An inability to retrieve information isn't the only cause of forgetting. Why are some memories lost so quickly?

Decay

Memory traces fade over time and lack of use.

Encoding Failure

Often, memory failures occur because <u>information wasn't stored in the first place</u>. It wasn't attended to at sensory or short-term memory and was not encoded and stored.

Interference

New information can prevent retrieval of old information (and vice versa). Events in the environment may prevent us from attending to the information and encoding it properly.

Sensory Memory

Sensory organs collect information that is retained for a short period of time. If the information is not attended to it is "forgotten."

Short-Term Memory (STM)

STM is a temporary storehouse for small amounts of information. If the information is not attended to, or if it is not sufficiently important, it is "forgotten." (See Encoding Failure.)

Long-Term Memory (LTM)

LTM is the large storehouse of relatively permanent information that was important to us in some way at one time. If the information is not attended to, or if it is not sufficiently important, it is "forgotten." (See Encoding Failure.)

Psychological Motives

Repression (unconscious) or suppression (conscious) of information may occur for psychological reasons.

Cue Dependency

Many of our memories rely on cues in the environment, including the bodily state that we are experiencing as we attempt to encode and store memories (state-dependent learning).

CHAPTER 9 Memory

Psychology on the Web

To link to the following sites, visit *www.psychology.wadsworth.com/coon_gateways10e*

Active Brain Areas in Working Memory
A three-dimensional MRI reconstruction of a person's brain while holding letters in working memory.

Exploratorium: Memory
Demonstrations and articles related to memory from an exceptional science museum.

False-Memory Test
Use the materials in this site to induce false memories in others (for demonstration purposes).

Memory Techniques and Mnemonics
Links to information on mnemonics.

Questions and Answers About Memories of Childhood Abuse
From APA, a summary of the repressed memory issue.

Repressed and Recovered Memories
Site devoted to the recovered memory controversy; has links to both sides of the controversy.

The Magical Number Seven, Plus or Minus Two
Full text of George Miller's original article.

Related Articles in InfoTrac College Edition
Go to *http://www.infotrac-college.com/wadsworth* and search by article number.

A98194161
Research shows where memories are made. (2003, March 3). *Pain & Central Nervous System Week*, p. 10.

A89160455
Ahlberg, S., & Sharps, M. (2002, June). Bartlett revisited: Reconfiguration of long-term memory in young and older adults. (Statistical data included.) *Journal of Genetic Psychology, 163*(2), 211(8).

A98594284
LeBoutillier, N., & Marks, D. (2003, February). Mental imagery and creativity: A meta-analytic review study. *British Journal of Psychology, 94*(1), 29(16).

A98922817
Davidhizar, R. (2003, January–March). When your memory malfunctions: Implications for the manager. *The Health Care Manager, 22*(1), 45(7).

A21249656
Myslinski, N. (1998, November). Now where did I put those keys? (Memory loss.) *World and I, 13*(11), 160(8).

Interactive Learning
Links to the *PsychNow!* and *Psyk.trek* CD-ROMs:

PsychNow! 2.0 5d. Memory Systems, 5e. Forgetting.

Psyk.trek 2.0 6a. Memory Encoding, 6b. Memory Storage, 6c. Physiology of Memory.

COGNITION, LANGUAGE, AND CREATIVITY

How we think, communicate, and problem solve are essential elements of being human.

Cognition

Thinking (cognition) is influenced by how the information is mentally represented, which can come in the form of:

- Images, which are often mental representations that have a picture-like quality.
- Concepts, which are ideas that represent a group of objects or events that allow us to think abstractly.
- Language, which includes words or symbols and the rules for combining them, is used for thinking and communication. Language is an especially powerful way to encode information and manipulate ideas.

Animal Cognition

Many animals appear to engage in elementary forms of thinking.

- Language is primarily a human characteristic.
- Animals are capable of rudimentary language use, but only with the aid of human intervention.

Errors in Thinking

Some common thinking errors can be avoided if you know the pitfalls of intuitive thought.

Problem Solving

Expert problem solving is based on acquired knowledge and strategies. Experts are not naturally smarter than novices.

CREATIVE THINKING

Creative thinking is novel, divergent, and tempered with a dash of practicality.

Creativity

Creativity can be enhanced by strategies that promote divergent thinking.

Break Mental Sets

A tendency to perceive a problem in a certain way is called a mental set and may impede problem solving.

Try Different Approaches

Restating the problem in different ways may enhance creativity.

Understanding

Understanding (deeper comprehension of a problem) is necessary to solve some problems.

Insights

Insights occur when answers appear suddenly, usually as a result of reorganizing the elements of the problem.

Heuristics

Heuristics are strategies that aid problem solving, especially by limiting the number of possible solutions to be tried.

Mechanical Solutions

Mechanical solutions may be achieved by trial and error or by rote. This strategy is how computers solve some problems.

Define Broadly

Often we restrict our creativity by focusing on a narrow aspect of a situation without considering a wider viewpoint.

Find Analogies

Look for analogies where similar problems exist and may have been solved.

CHAPTER **10** Cognition, Language, and Creativity

Psychology on the Web

To link to the following sites, visit *www.psychology.wadsworth.com/coon_gateways10e*

Creativity Web
Multiple links to resources on creativity.

The Psychology of Invention
An exploration of how invention and discovery happen.

The Question of Primate Language
This article from the National Zoo discusses primate communication and intelligence.

Related Articles in InfoTrac College Edition

Go to *http://www.infotrac-college.com/wadsworth* and search by article number.

A64692527
Neuman, Y., Leibowitz, L., & Schwarz, B. (2000, Spring). Patterns of verbal mediation during problem solving: A sequential analysis of self-explanation. *The Journal of Experimental Education, 68*(3), 197.

A58724834
Toal, M. (1999, May). The ants come marching. (Ant communication.) *Highlights for Children, 54*(5), 8.

A98254108
AI agent application 1.0. (Internet focus.) (KazTrix AI agent.) (2003, February). *Database and Network Journal, 33*(1), 20(1).

A93532586
Gelade, G. (2002, August). Creative style, personality, and artistic endeavor. *Genetic, Social, and General Psychology Monographs, 128*(3), 213(22).

A95501260
Subbotsky, E., & Quinteros, G. (2002, November). Do cultural factors affect causal beliefs? Rational and magical thinking in Britain and Mexico. *British Journal of Psychology, 93*(4), 519(25).

Interactive Learning

Links to the *PsychNow!* and *Psyk.trek* CD-ROMs:

PsychNow! 2.0 5f. Cognition and Language, 5g. Problem Solving and Creativity.

Psyk.trek 2.0 6d. Problem Solving, 6e. Decision Making.

Photo: AP/Wide World Photos

INTELLIGENCE

An overall capacity to think rationally, act purposefully, and deal effectively with the environment is a common definition of intelligence.

Heredity vs. Environment

Both heredity and environment influence intelligence, but only improved social conditions and education (environment) can raise intelligence.

Retardation

Most people who are mentally retarded can master basic adaptive behaviors, and with support, they can find a place in the community.

Average IQ

Most people score in the mid-range (90–109) on intelligence tests. Only a small percentage of people have exceptionally high and low IQ scores.

High IQ

A high IQ does not automatically lead to high achievement. A high IQ reveals potential, but it does not guarantee success.

Aptitudes

Everyone has special aptitudes (capacities for learning certain abilities) and potentials. Those who possess a wide range of mental abilities are above average in intelligence.

Intelligence Testing

Intelligence tests provide a useful but narrow estimate of real-world intelligence.

Familial Retardation

In 30 to 40 percent of cases of retardation, no known biological problem can be identified. Generally this occurs in impoverished environments where nutrition, intellectual stimulation, medical care, and emotional support may have been lacking.

Organic Retardation

Approximately half of mental retardation is related to organic or physical disorders, including:
- Birth injuries (such as lack of oxygen during delivery)
- Fetal damage (such as mother's use of drugs or alcohol)
- Metabolic disorders (in which energy production and use within the body is affected)
- Genetic abnormalities (missing or extra chromosomes)
- Environmental circumstances (poor nutrition, ingestion of lead or other toxins)

Real-World Intelligence

Real-world intelligence combines a fast nervous system with learned knowledge and skills and an acquired ability to manage one's own thinking and problem solving.

Intelligence Quotient (IQ)

Classical IQ is a calculation in which an individual's chronological age (expected performance) is compared with his or her mental age (actual performance level).

Calculating IQ

A child who is 10 years old and who performs at a 12-year-old's level is said to have an IQ of 120. (Mental age divided by chronological age yields 1.2, which is multiplied by 100.)

Cultural Validity

Traditional IQ tests are not universally valid for all cultural groups.

Traditional IQ Tests

Traditional IQ tests measure linguistic, logical, mathematical, and spatial abilities. It is likely that we all use other types of intelligence in daily life.

Cultural-Fair Tests

Culture-fair tests minimize the importance of skills and knowledge that may be more common in some cultures than in others. They have been developed to avoid biases in test construction.

Psychology on the Web

To link to the following sites, visit *www.psychology.wadsworth.com/ coon_gateways10e*

Be Careful How You Define Intelligence
An article about cross-cultural differences in intelligence.

Helping Your Highly Gifted Child
Advice for parents of gifted children.

Introduction to Mental Retardation
Answers to basic questions about mental retardation.

IQ Tests
These sites provide links to a number of IQ tests.

The Bell Curve Flattened
An article that summarizes objections to *The Bell Curve*.

The Knowns and Unknowns of Intelligence
What is known about intelligence and intelligence tests, from the APA.

Related Articles in InfoTrac College Edition

Go to *http://www.infotrac-college.com/wadsworth* and search by article number.

A53560431
Deary, I. (1998, December 19). Differences in mental abilities. (Clinical review.) *British Medical Journal, 317*(7174), 1701(3).

A97997817
Bower, B. (2003, February 8). Essence of g: Scientists search for the biology of smarts. (General factor used to determine intelligence level.) *Science News, 163*(6), 92(2).

A87103152
Alexander, D. (2002, May). The surgeon general focuses the nation on health and mental retardation. (Surgeon General Special Report.) *The Exceptional Parent, 32*(5), 28(8).

A74571884
Fasko, D., Jr. (2001, April). An analysis of multiple intelligences theory and its use with the gifted and talented. *Roeper Review, 23*(3), 126.

A14106792
Solomon, C. M. (1993, March). Testing is not at odds with diversity efforts. *Personnel Journal, 72*(3), 100(5). Bus.Coll.: 70S5156.

Interactive Learning

Links to the *Psyk.trek* CD-ROM:

Psyk.trek 2.0 7. Testing and Intelligence.

Photo: Kaluzny-Thatcher/Getty Images

MOTIVATION AND EMOTION

Motives and goals greatly influence what we do and how we use our energies. Motivated behavior is also influenced by learned habits, external cues, and cultural values.

Motivation

The concept of motivation refers to the ways in which our actions are <u>initiated</u>, <u>sustained</u>, and <u>directed</u>.

Primary Motives

Basic motives, such as hunger and thirst, are controlled by internal signals monitored within the brain. Primary motives are based on biological requirements for survival.

Secondary Motives

Many needs and motives are learned. We learn how to achieve praise, money, success, and a variety of other reinforcers that fulfill our goals and desires.

Emotion

Emotion is a state characterized by:
• Physiological arousal
• Outward behaviors (facial expressions, gestures, and so forth)
• Subjective feelings
Emotions can be disruptive, but overall they help us adapt to environmental challenges.

Emotional Intelligence

People who are "smart" emotionally are self-aware and empathetic. They understand emotions; can manage their feelings; and use emotions to enhance thinking, decision making, and relationships.

Primary Emotions

Robert Plutchik's research indicates eight primary emotions, each of which may vary in intensity:
• Fear
• Surprise
• Sadness
• Disgust
• Anger
• Anticipation
• Joy
• Acceptance

FOOD AND EATING

• Hunger is a basic physiological need.
• <u>Overeating</u> and <u>undereating</u> are often related to emotional or cultural factors.

Eating Disorders

<u>Anorexia nervosa</u> (active self-starvation) and <u>bulimia nervosa</u> (binge-purge eating) are serious disorders that can cause serious physical damage or death.

Diet

• A diet is not just something meant to help a person lose weight.
• A person's current diet is defined by the types and amounts of food regularly eaten and the content of the foods.
• The most effective "diet" is one that changes eating habits and activity levels.

Stimulus Motives

- Numerous activities are related to our needs for stimulation and our efforts to maintain comfortable levels of arousal.
- Stimulus motives appear to be innate, but they are not strictly necessary for survival. They include curiosity, exploration, and physical contact.

Elements of Love

According to Robert Sternberg's triangular theory, love is made up of three elements. In its ideal form, romantic love is a combination of:
- Passion
- Intimacy
- Commitment

However, many long-term relationships are built on companionship, intimacy, mutual respect, shared interests, and firm friendship.

Psychology on the Web

To link to the following sites, visit *www.psychology.wadsworth.com/coon_gateways10e*

Controlling Anger
From the APA, this page discusses anger and some strategies for its control.

Eating Disorders Web Site
Home page of a self-help group for those afflicted with eating disorders.

Emotions and Emotional Intelligence
An online bibliography in the area of emotions and emotional intelligence, describing current research findings and notes of interest.

Gestures Around the World
A description of body language practices in a variety of cultures (available by free subscription).

Research on Human Emotions
Links to a variety of sources on emotion.

The Validity of Polygraph Examinations
From the APA, information about the doubtful validity of polygraph examinations.

Scientific Validity of Polygraph Examinations
From the U.S. Congress Office of Technology Assessment.

Related Articles in InfoTrac College Edition

Go to *http://www.infotrac-college.com/wadsworth* and search by article number.

A97329152
Dolezal, S., Mohan Welsh, L., Pressley, M., & Vincent, M. (2003, January). How nine third-grade teachers motivate student academic engagement. *The Elementary School Journal, 103*(3), 239(30).

A98045519
Geller, J., Srikameswaran, S., Zaitsoff, S., Cockell, S., & Poole, G. (2003, April). Mothers' and fathers' perceptions of their adolescent daughters' shape, weight, and body esteem: Are they accurate? *Journal of Youth and Adolescence, 32*(2), 81(7).

A55017659
Bradizza, C., Reifman, A., & Barnes, G. (1999, July). Social and coping reasons for drinking: Predicting alcohol misuse in adolescents. *Journal of Studies on Alcohol, 60*(4), 491.

A94595099
Developing your emotional intelligence. (Interpersonal skills.) (2002, November). *Essential Assistant, 15*(11), 8(1).

A98688392
Renew passion, intimacy and romance in your relationship: Join the 'Love Boat Cruise for Relationship Workshops'. (2003, March 13). *PR Newswire,* p. NYFNSF0313032003.

Interactive Learning

Links to the *PsychNow!* and *Psyk.trek* CD-ROMs:

PsychNow! 2.0 6a. Motivation, 6b. Emotion.

Psyk.trek 2.0 8a. Hunger, 8b. Achievement Motivation, 8c. Elements of Emotion, 8d. Theories of Emotion, 4a. Biological Rhythms.

Photo: © Mark Richards/PhotoEdit

GENDER AND SEXUALITY

Male and female are not simple either/or categories.

Sex

- <u>Sex</u> refers to whether you are biologically male or female.
- The sexual and reproductive organs are referred to as <u>primary sexual characteristics.</u>
- More superficial physical features that appear at puberty in response to hormonal signals from the pituitary gland are referred to as <u>secondary sexual characteristics.</u>

Gender

- <u>Gender</u> refers to all the psychological and social characteristics associated with being male or female.
- Your personal, private sense of being female or male is your <u>gender (sexual) identity</u> and is usually formed by the time you are 3 or 4 years old.
- Sexual identity is complex, multifaceted, and influenced by biology, socialization, and learning.

Androgyny

The presence of both masculine and feminine traits in a single person is referred to as <u>androgyny</u>. It is possible, and generally desirable, to have both masculine and feminine gender traits.

Sexual Orientation

- The degree to which you are attracted emotionally and erotically to members of the same or opposite sex determines your <u>sexual orientation.</u>
- Similar factors (heredity, biology, and socialization) underlie all sexual orientations.

Sexual Adjustment

Solutions exist for many sexual adjustment problems, but good communication and healthy relationships are the real keys to sexual satisfaction.

Sexual Behaviors

Adults normally engage in a wide variety of sexual behaviors. However, coercive and/or compulsive sexual behaviors are emotionally unhealthy.

Male/Female Differences

Women and men are more alike than they are different. The core of humanity in each person is more important than superficial gender differences.

Sexual Arousal

An understanding of human sexual response contributes to responsible and satisfying sexual behavior.

Safe Sex

Each person must take responsibility for practicing safe sex and for choosing when, where, and with whom to express his or her sexuality.

Touching

- Direct stimulation of the erogenous zones (areas of the body that produce pleasure and/or provoke erotic desire) is a key ingredient of arousal.
- Most touching is nonsexual. However, touching tends to be highly restricted in North America because of social norms and fears that touching will be perceived as erotic or inappropriate.

Psychology on the Web

To link to the following sites, visit *www.psychology.wadsworth.com/coon_gateways10e*

"Friends" Raping Friends
Information about date rape.

Go Ask Alice
The Sexual Health section of this site offers valuable information and links about sexuality.

Online Sexual Disorders Screening Test for Men
A self-scoring test for male sexual problems.

Online Sexual Disorders Screening Test for Women
A self-scoring test for female sexual problems.

Preventing HIV Infection
Advice on how to prevent HIV infection, provided by the United Nations Population Fund.

Sexual Orientation and Homosexuality—FAQ
Answers basic questions about sexual orientation and homosexuality, provided by the APA.

Related Articles in InfoTrac College Edition

Go to *http://www.infotrac-college.com/wadsworth* and search by article number.

A90446367
Bailey, J. M., Bechtold, K., & Berenbaum, S. (2002, August). Who are tomboys and why should we study them? *Archives of Sexual Behavior, 31*(4), 333(9).

A97892383
Alexander, G. (2003, February). An evolutionary perspective of sex-typed toy preferences: Pink, blue, and the brain. *Archives of Sexual Behavior, 32*(1), 7(8). (Author's abstract Plenum Publishing Corporation.)

A97070710
Prevalence of women's sex problems overestimated, study says. (2003, February 6). *Women's Health Weekly,* p. 31.

A89831450
Feiring, C., Deblinger, E., Hoch-Espada, A., & Haworth, T. (2002, October). Romantic relationship aggression and attitudes in high school students: The role of gender, grade, and attachment and emotional styles. (Statistical data included.) *Journal of Youth and Adolescence, 31*(5), 373(13).

A82013897
Renaud, C., & Byers, S. (2001, August). Positive and negative sexual cognitions: Subjective experience and relationships to sexual adjustment. (Statistical data included.) *The Journal of Sex Research, 38*(3), 252(11).

Interactive Learning

Links to the *PsychNow!* CD-ROM:

PsychNow! 2.0 6e. Human Sexuality, 8g. Gender and Stereotyping.

PERSONALITY

Each of us displays consistent behavior patterns that define our own personalities and allow us to predict how other people will act.

Character

Character and personality are not the same thing. The term character implies a judgment about desirability or undesirability.

Personality Types

A personality type refers to people who have several traits in common (such as strong, silent, athletic, and so on).

Understanding Personality

Personality can be understood by:
- Identifying traits
- Probing mental conflicts and dynamics
- Noting the effects of prior learning and social situations
- Knowing how people perceive themselves

Personality Traits

Personality traits are stable qualities that a person shows in most situations. Traits are inferred from behaviors and are often used to predict future behaviors (such as shy, sensitive, orderly, and so on).

Personality Testing

To measure and assess personality, psychologists use:
- Interviews
- Direct observation
- Questionnaires
- Projective tests

Self-Concept

A person's perception of his or her own personality traits is referred to as self-concept. Self-concepts have a significant impact on our behaviors.

Personality Theories

- Trait theories: Many personality tests are based on trait theories.
- Psychoanalytic theories: Based on the works of Sigmund Freud.
- Behavioristic theories: Seek to determine what makes learning experiences have a lasting effect.
- Humanistic theories: Focus on human problems, potentials, ideals, and the ability to change.

Changing Personality

Shyness is related to public self-consciousness and other psychological factors that can be altered, thereby helping some people overcome shyness. A goal of therapy is to assist in changing personality.

Classifying Traits

Traits are often described as being:
- <u>Common</u> (those shared by most members of a culture)
- <u>Individual</u> (which define a person's unique personal qualities)
- <u>Cardinal</u> (a trait so basic that all of a person's activities can be traced to that trait)

Note: Very few of us possess cardinal traits.

Self-Monitoring

Our behavior is influenced by <u>self-monitoring</u>, the process of observing, regulating, and controlling the personal image we display to others.

High or Low Self-Monitors

Some of us are <u>high self-monitors</u> (actively seeking to change the impression we make to fit situations and expectations) while others are <u>low self-monitors</u> (seeking to faithfully express who we are regardless of the situation).

CHAPTER 14 Personality

Psychology on the Web

To link to the following sites, visit *www.psychology.wadsworth.com/coon_gateways10e*

About Humanistic Psychology
Discusses the history and future of humanistic psychology.

FAQ About Psychological Tests
Answers to commonly asked questions about tests and testing, provided by the APA.

Freud Archives
Provided by the New York Psychoanalytic Institute and Society, this collection of links points to Internet resources related to Sigmund Freud and his works.

Personality and IQ Tests
Multiple links to personality tests and IQ tests that are scored online.

Related Articles in InfoTrac College Edition

Go to *http://www.infotrac-college.com/wadsworth* and search by article number.

A96399117
Pinker, S. (2003, January 20). Are your genes to blame? For your good looks? Sure. For your shyness or your temper? Not entirely. *Time, 161*(3), 98+.

A95259679
Millikan, E., Wamboldt, M., & Bihun, J. (2002, December). Perceptions of the family, personality characteristics, and adolescent internalizing symptoms. *Journal of the American Academy of Child and Adolescent Psychiatry, 41*(12), 1486(9).

A94080874
Guterl, F. (2002, November 11). What Freud got right: His theories, long discredited, are finding support from neurologists using modern brain imaging. *Newsweek,* p. 50. Mag.Coll.: 112C0873. Bus.Coll.: 143N2283.

A58119450
Janssen, T., & Carton, J. (1999, December). The effects of locus of control and task difficulty on procrastination. *Journal of Genetic Psychology, 160*(4), 436(7).

A55683969
Lilienfeld, S. (1999, September–October). Projective measures of personality and psychopathology: How well do they work? *Skeptical Inquirer, 23*(5), 32(8).

Interactive Learning

Links to the *PsychNow!* and *Psyk.trek* CD-ROMs:

PsychNow! 2.0 7a. Theories of Personality, 7e. Assessment.

Psyk.trek 2.0 10. Personality Theory.

HEALTH, STRESS, AND COPING

A variety of personal habits and behavior patterns affect health.

Stress, Stressors, and Pressure

- Stress is the mental and physical condition that occurs when a person must adjust or adapt to the environment.
- A stressor is the condition or event in the environment that challenges or threatens a person.
- Pressure occurs when a person must meet urgent external demands or expectations (when there is a deadline or a short period to make a response to a stressor).

Stress

Stress is a normal part of life. However, it is also a major risk factor for illness and disease.

People vs. Environment

- Although some events are more stressful than others are, stress always represents an interaction between people and the environments in which they live.
- Personality characteristics affect the amount of stress a person experiences and the subsequent risk of illness.

Behavioral Risk Factors

Maintaining good health is a personal responsibility, not a matter of luck. Wellness is based on minimizing risk factors and engaging in health-promoting behaviors.

Immune Reactions

The body's reactions to stress can directly damage internal organs, and stress impairs the body's immune system, increasing susceptibility to disease.

Appraising Stressors

Is the stressor a <u>threat</u> or a <u>challenge</u>? Our personal appraisal of an external event greatly affects the amount of stress we perceive.

Good Stress

Stress is not necessarily "bad." Some forms of stress are related to positive activities such as engaging in recreational activities, dating, or moving to a sought-after job. This form of "good" stress is called <u>eustress</u>.

Stress Reduction

- The damaging effects of stress can be reduced with stress management techniques.
- <u>Exercise</u>, <u>meditation</u>, <u>progressive relaxation</u>, and <u>modification of ineffective behaviors</u> allow us to manage stress more effectively.

Psychology on the Web

To link to the following sites, visit *www.psychology.wadsworth.com/ coon_gateways10e*

Burnout Test
A short questionnaire on job burnout.

Coping with Terrorism
Information about emotional reactions to terrorism, provided by the APA.

Focus on Stress
Strategies for reducing stress at work, including a weekly newsletter created by TalkAboutStress.com.

HealthyWay
A set of pages on health, nutrition, addictions, disabilities, sexuality, fitness, and much more.

Preventive Health Center
A general source of information on how to maintain health and prevent disease.

Stress Management: Review of Principles
Presents the core concepts of stress management education.

Stress, Anxiety, Fears, and Psychosomatic Disorders
A comprehensive source on stress, anxiety, and related disorders.

Type A Behavior
Describes Type A behavior, with links to an online test and related sites.

Related Articles in InfoTrac College Edition

Go to *http://www.infotrac-college.com/wadsworth* and search by article number.

A18486973
Birkimer, J., Druen, P., Holland, J., & Zingman, M. (1996, April). Predictors of health behavior from a behavior-analytic orientation. *The Journal of Social Psychology, 136*(2), 181(9).

A98540677
There's help for the workplace in stress-filled times. (2003, March 1). *HR Briefing*, p. 1(2).

A87774118
Pellitteri, J. (2002, March). The relationship between emotional intelligence and ego defense mechanisms. *The Journal of Psychology, 136*(2), 182(13). (Abstract.)

A94930857
Jackson, T., Weiss, K., Lundquist, J., & Soderlind, A. (2002, September). Perceptions of goal directed activities of optimists and pessimists: A personal projects analysis. *The Journal of Psychology, 136*(5), 521(12).

A96305931
Tacon, A., McComb, J., Caldera, Y., & Randolph, P. (2003, January–March). Mindfulness meditation, anxiety reduction, and heart disease: A pilot study. *Family and Community Health, 26*(1), 25(9).

Interactive Learning

Links to the *PsychNow!* and *Psyk.trek* CD-ROMs:

PsychNow! 2.0 6c. Coping with Emotion, 6d. Stress and Health.

Psyk.trek 2.0 11f. Types of Stress, 11g. Responding to Stress.

PSYCHOLOGICAL DISORDERS

Psychological disorders <u>damage the quality of life</u>, in varying degrees, for many people. Psychological disorders are complex and have multiple causes.

Psychopathology

Psychopathology—which involves <u>identifying</u>, <u>classifying</u>, and <u>explaining psychological disorders</u>—is worthwhile and necessary.

Insanity

Insanity is a <u>legal term</u> referring to a mental inability to manage one's own affairs or to be aware of the consequences of one's actions.

What Is Normal?

Determining abnormality can be tricky. Several factors may be taken into consideration before a diagnosis is made:

- How unhappy or anxious a person may feel (<u>subjective discomfort</u>)
- How far from the center of a distribution curve regarding some facet of life a person may be (<u>statistical abnormality</u>)
- Whether the behavior is consistent with the social norms (<u>social nonconformity</u>)
- How difficult is it for a person to adapt to the demands of day-to-day life (<u>maladaptiveness</u>)

Risk Factors

Several factors may contribute to various instances of psychopathology:

- <u>Social conditions</u> (poverty, stressful living conditions, social disorganization)
- <u>Family factors</u> (poor or immature parenting, marital strife)
- <u>Psychological factors</u> (stress, learning disorders)
- <u>Biological factors</u> (genetic defects, poor prenatal care, exposure to toxic chemicals or drugs)

SUICIDE

Suicide is a relatively common cause of death that can, in many cases, be prevented.

Statistics

Suicide is the seventh leading cause of death in North America. For every two people who die in a homicide, three take their own lives.

Prevention

Knowing the common characteristics of suicidal thoughts and feelings will give you some guidance in talking to a suicidal person. Your most important task may be to <u>establish rapport</u> with the person while offering support, acceptance, and caring.

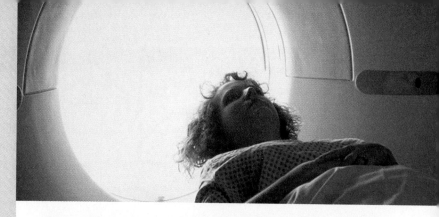

Classifying Mental Disorders

The most widely used classification system is the *Diagnostic and Statistical Manual of Mental Disorders* (DSM-IV-TR, 2000). This manual:

- Standardizes terminology for mental health workers
- Organizes mental disorders into categories
- Provides available information concerning statistical data
- Establishes criteria and assists workers in making a diagnosis

The Medical Model

The medical model treats human psychological behaviors as "diseases" with "symptoms" that can be "cured." Despite its value, the medical model of psychological disorders sometimes leads to a limited view of human behavior and problems.

Personality Disorders

- Maladaptive behavior patterns, unhealthy personality types, and excessive levels of anxiety underlie many mental disorders.
- These deeply ingrained patterns of behavior are considered personality disorders. Panic attacks, obsessive-compulsive behaviors, posttraumatic stress reactions, and multiple personalities are included.

Maladaptive Behavior

Psychologically unhealthy behavior is maladaptive and involves a loss of adequate control over thoughts, feelings, and actions.

Psychosis

- The most severe forms of psychopathology involve emotional extremes and/or a break with reality.
- Typical psychotic episodes can include hallucinations, delusions, disturbed communication and disintegration of the personality, mania, depression, and schizophrenia.

Psychology on the Web

To link to the following sites, visit *www.psychology.wadsworth.com/coon_gateways10e*

A Guide to Depressive and Manic Depressive Illness
An overview of mood disorders, their diagnosis, and treatment.

Anxiety Disorders Association of America
General information about anxiety disorders.

Anxiety Disorders
From the National Institute of Mental Health, a brief overview of the symptoms and treatment of the major anxiety disorders, including information and links to sites about anxiety disorders.

Depression After Delivery
A site devoted to providing information about postpartum depression.

DSM-IV Questions and Answers
Answers to common questions about the DSM-IV from its source, the APA.

Internet Mental Health
Comprehensive page on mental health, with links to many other sites.

National Alliance for the Mentally Ill
Home page of NAMI, which includes information and links.

National Institute of Mental Health
This site provides links to public information, news and events, and research activities.

Personality Disorders
Multiple links to information on personality disorders and their treatment.

Understanding Schizophrenia
From the National Institute of Mental Health, an online booklet providing an extensive look at schizophrenia.

Related Articles in InfoTrac College Edition

Go to *http://www.infotrac-college.com/wadsworth* and search by article number.

A89146370
Lahey, B., Loeber, R., Burke, J., & Rathouz, P. (2002, August). Adolescent outcomes of childhood conduct disorder among clinic-referred boys: Predictors of improvement. *Journal of Abnormal Child Psychology, 30*(4), 333(16).

A96074497
Brain scans may detect early stages of psychosis. (2002, December 23). *Mental Health Weekly, 12*(48), 6(1).

A98194162
Study suggests three times more Americans than earlier believed may be affected. (2003, March 3). *Pain & Central Nervous System Week*, p. 11.

A98730457
Forecast: Sales of antipsychotics and anticonvulsants to hit $2.6B in 2011. (2003, March 17). *Health & Medicine Week*, p. 11.

A98881751
Alarming stats for elderly depression and suicide: Teach signs and symptoms of depression. (2003, March). *Patient Education Management, 10*(3), 28(3).

Interactive Learning

Links to the *PsychNow!* and *Psyk.trek* CD-ROMs:

PsychNow! 2.0 7c. Abnormality and Psychopathology, 7d. Nonpsychotic, Psychotic, and Affective Disorders.

Psyk.trek 2.0 Clinical Diagnosis (simulation), 11a. Anxiety Disorders, 11b. Mood Disorders, 11c. Schizophrenic Disorders.

Photo: © Matthew Borkoski/Index Stock Imagery/PictureQuest

THERAPIES

Psychotherapy facilitates positive changes in personality, behavior, and adjustment.

Origins of Therapy

Before the development of modern therapies, superstition dominated attempts to treat psychological problems.

Seeking Help

Everyone should know how to obtain high-quality mental health care in his or her community. Most communities have a variety of services available.

- The yellow pages will list psychologists, psychiatrists, and counselors.
- Public mental health services often provide services directly and can make referrals to private therapists.
- Mental health associations are often organized by concerned citizens who keep listings of qualified therapists and services.
- Crises hotlines are staffed by volunteers trained to provide information about resources available.

Therapy Approaches

Five major categories of psychotherapy are:

1. Psychodynamic (based on Freud's theories)
2. Insight (clients achieve a deeper understanding of their thoughts, emotions, and behaviors)
3. Behavioral (the principles of learning and conditioning are used to make constructive changes in behavior)
4. Cognitive (efforts are directed at changing maladaptive thoughts, beliefs, and feelings)
5. Group therapies (make therapeutic use of group dynamics)

How Effective Is Therapy?

Psychotherapy is generally effective, although no single form of therapy is superior to others.

Medical Treatments

All medical treatments for psychological disorders have pros and cons. Overall, however, their effectiveness is improving.

Self-Management

Some personal problems can be successfully treated by using self-management techniques.

CHAPTER

17 Therapies

Psychology on the Web

To link to the following sites, visit *www.psychology.wadsworth.com/ coon_gateways10e*

Basics of Cognitive Therapy
An overview of cognitive therapy, with suggested readings.

How to Find Help for Life's Problems
Provides information on psychotherapy and advice on how to choose a psychotherapist.

NetPsychology
Explores the delivery of psychological services on the Internet.

Psychological Self-Help
An online book about self-improvement.

The Effectiveness of Psychotherapy
A summary of a *Consumer Reports* survey on the effectiveness of psychotherapy.

Types of Therapies
Describes four different approaches to therapy and includes information about choosing a therapist.

La Chaise Lounge Web Counselor
An online advice column presenting typical personal problems along with examples of advice.

Related Articles in InfoTrac College Edition

Go to *http://www.infotrac-college.com/wadsworth* and search by article number.

A94206286
Psychotherapies: Can we tell the difference? (2002, October). *Harvard Mental Health Letter, 19*(4), 0.

A65133413
Johnston, M. (1999, December). On becoming non-judgmental: Some difficulties for an ethics of counseling. *Journal of Medical Ethics, 25*(6), 487.

A97724109
Expert explores psychosocial interventions for ADHD. (2003, February). *The Brown University Child and Adolescent Behavior Letter, 19*(2), 1(4).

A95259671
Manassis, K., Mendlowitz, S., Scapillato, D., Avery, D., Fiksenbaum, L., Freire, M., Monga, S., & Owens, M. (2002, December). Group and individual cognitive-behavioral therapy for childhood anxiety disorders: A randomized trial. *Journal of the American Academy of Child and Adolescent Psychiatry, 41*(12), 1423(8).

A95056392
Walsh, N. (2002, November). Kids' depression: SSRI data grow. (Two double-blind studies.) *Clinical Psychiatry News, 30*(11), 20(1).

Interactive Learning

Links to the *PsychNow!* and *Psyk.trek* CD-ROMs:

PsychNow! 2.0 7b. Major Psychological Therapies.

Psyk.trek 2.0 11d. Insight Therapies, 11e. Behavioral and Biomedical Therapies.

SOCIAL BEHAVIOR

Social psychology studies how we behave, think, and feel in social situations.

Social Groups

We are born into an organized society with established values, expectations, and behavior patterns. Each person in a society is a member of many overlapping social groups.

Group Norms

Within groups there are accepted (often unspoken) standards for behavior.

Group Roles

Social roles (patterns of behavior expected of persons in various social positions) may be:
- Ascribed (not under our control) or
- Achieved (roles we have chosen for ourselves)

Structure and Cohesion

Structure (the network of roles, communication, and power in a group) and cohesiveness (the degree of attraction among group members and our desire to remain members of the group) influence our behaviors within groups.

Attribution Theory

Social behavior cannot be fully understood unless we know what causes people attribute their behavior to and how they explain the behavior of others.

Fundamental Attribution Error

We seldom know the reasons for the actions of other people. The most common error is to attribute other's behaviors to internal causes (someone is impatient due to a character flaw) when much of a person's behavior is based on external causes (they are impatient because of being late for an important appointment).

Affiliation

A basic human trait is a desire to associate with other people. Many social interactions can be understood as an exchange of attention, information, affection, or favors between two people.

Interpersonal Attraction

We are attracted to other people—even potential mates—for reasons that are predictable and fairly universal.

Personal Space

The nature of many relationships is revealed by the distance a person is comfortable maintaining between self and another person. Each of us maintains personal space, which is an extension of ourselves past the skin and into the environment.

Social Influence

A major fact of social life is that our behavior is influenced in numerous ways by the actions of other people. Our desire to remain part of a group may overcome our better judgment.

Conformity and Obedience

Everyone is affected by pressure to conform, obey, and comply. There are times when it is valuable to know how to recognize and resist such pressures.

Assertiveness Training

Assertiveness is a valuable alternative to becoming aggressive or being victimized in social situations.

Misguided Group Behavior

A number of social problems are based on social traps—situations that provide immediate rewards for actions that have damaging effects in the long run.

Psychology on the Web

To link to the following sites, visit *www.psychology.wadsworth.com/coon_gateways10e*

Social Psychology Network
A comprehensive site with many links to information about social psychology.

In Your Face
A paper that discusses research on facial attractiveness.

Center for Evolutionary Psychology
A University of California—Santa Barbara group offering information on research in training in evolutionary psychology, including a primer, a reading list, and links.

Evolutionary Psychology for the Common Person
Provides a thorough introduction to evolutionary psychology, with links to other information on EP.

Preventing Groupthink
A slide presentation that offers five ways to prevent groupthink.

Social Psychology Humor
A project of a Miami University class, this page has links to cartoons that relate to principles of social psychology.

Related Articles in InfoTrac College Edition

Go to *http://www.infotrac-college.com/wadsworth* and search by article number.

A8621274
Barker, R., & Pearce, C. G. (1990, July). The importance of proxemics at work. (space and human comfort in the work environment). *Supervisory Management, 35*(7), 10(2).

A18534479
Kilbury, R., Bordieri, J., & Wong, H. (1996, April–June). Impact of physical disability and gender on personal space. *The Journal of Rehabilitation, 62*(2), 59(3).

A21123352
Amirkhan, J. (1998, September). Attributions as predictors of coping and distress. *Personality & Social Psychology Bulletin, 24*(9), 1006(13).

A91718072
Sorkin, A. (2002, October). I knew I was in love with her when . . . : Every man knows that moment when a woman wins his heart. Here, some awww-inspiring stories. *Marie Claire, 9*(10), 171(3).

A94335088
Coleman, S. (2002, Spring). A test for the effect of conformity on crime rates using voter turnout. *The Sociological Quarterly, 43*(2), 257(21).

Interactive Learning

Links to the *PsychNow!* and *Psyk.trek* CD-ROMs:

PsychNow! 2.0 8b. Attribution, 8c. Social Influence.

Psyk.trek 2.0 12a. Attribution Processes.

ATTITUDES, CULTURE, AND HUMAN RELATIONS

- Attitudes subtly affect nearly all aspects of social behavior.
- Our interpersonal and intercultural relations are affected by attitudes.

Persuasion

- Persuasion is any deliberate attempt to change attitudes or beliefs through information and arguments.
- To persuade others, a person must be aware of his or her role as a communicator, the characteristics of the audience, and the type of message that will appeal to them.

Brainwashing

Forced attitude change (brainwashing) is sometimes used by cults and other coercive groups.

Attitudes That Injure

Prejudice, discrimination, intolerance, and stereotyping damage the lives of many people.

Attitudes

- Attitudes are mixtures of belief and emotion that summarize our evaluations of people, objects, or institutions.
- Attitudes predispose us to behave in positive or negative ways.

Helping Others

Understanding and removing barriers to prosocial behavior can encourage acts of helping and altruism.

Sociobiology

- Evolutionary psychology attributes some aspects of human behavior to the challenges of survival and reproduction our distant ancestors faced.
- Sociobiology, an extreme form of evolutionary psychology, argues that competition, war, aggression, fear of strangers, and many other behaviors have become imbedded in our genes.

Living with Diversity

Multicultural harmony is attainable through conscious efforts to be more tolerant.

Reducing Prejudice

Prejudice is reduced by equal-status contact with other groups and by mutual interdependence, which promotes cooperation.

Superordinate Goals

Superordinate goals exist when one goal (such as facing a common threat in order to survive) exceeds or overrides all other goals (people set aside petty goals and differences in the face of natural disasters).

Equal Status

Equal-status contact involves social interaction on an equal footing, without obvious differences in power or status.

Aggression

Aggression is a fact of life, but humans are not inevitably aggressive.

Psychology on the Web

To link to the following sites, visit *www.psychology.wadsworth.com/ coon_gateways10e*

Information About Cults and Psychological Manipulation
Provides research and resources about psychological manipulation, cult groups, sects, and new religious movements.

Ethnic Images in the Comics
Articles on the history of ethnic stereotyping in the comics, originally from an exhibition at the Museum of the Balch Institute for Ethnic Studies in Philadelphia.

Implicit Association Test (1)
Online tests from Project Implicit, Understanding Prejudice, and Tolerance.org that purportedly reveal the unconscious roots of prejudice.

Social Psychology Network
The self-proclaimed "largest social psychology database on the Internet," this comprehensive site has more than 5,000 links to information about social psychology.

Violence on Television
Provided by the APA, this page discusses research on and the implications of watching television violence.

Related Articles in InfoTrac College Edition

Go to *http://www.infotrac-college.com/wadsworth* and search by article number.

A80856267
Chow, P., & Wood, W. (2001, Fall). Comparing cognitive dissonance test scores of college students in Canada with those in the United States. *Education, 122*(1), 128(3).

A91394545
Larimer, T. (2002, July 8). Cult shock: Yearning for spiritual leadership, Japan has spawned a rash of apocalyptic religions and ominously popular sects. *Time International, 159*(26), 24+.

A92523638
Massachusetts exit exam is discriminatory, suit alleges. (2002, September 25). *Special Education Report, 28*(20), 7(1).

A96125690
Kuttne, R. (2003, January 13). Having it both ways on race. *The American Prospect, 13*(24), 2(2).

A98731064
Genes and the environment have a significant effect on aggression. (2003, March 20). *Women's Health Weekly,* p. 43.

Interactive Learning

Links to the *PsychNow!* and *Psyk.trek* CD-ROMs:

PsychNow! 2.0 8a. Helping Others, 8d. Attitudes and Prejudice, 8e. Aggression.

Psyk.trek 2.0 12c. Attitude Change, 12d. Prejudice.

APPLIED PSYCHOLOGY

Applied psychology refers to the use of psychological principles and research methods to solve practical problems. The largest applied areas are clinical and counseling psychology, but there are many others.

Sports Psychology

Sports psychologists enhance sports performance and the value of participating in sports. Sports psychologists assist athletes by teaching them to relax, ignore distractions, or cope with their emotions to attain peak performances.

Industrial-Organizational (I-O) Psychology

I-O psychologists enhance the quality of work by matching people with jobs and by improving human relations at work.

Management Theory

Effective management at work must take human behavior into account.

Space Psychology

Space habitats magnify many of the psychological challenges we face in daily life. Living in space has provided valuable lessons about how we can live in greater harmony here on earth.

The Law and Psychology

Psychological factors greatly affect the law and jury decisions.

Environmental Psychology

Environmental psychologists study the relationship between environments and human behavior.

Educational Psychology

Educational psychologists seek to understand how people learn and how teachers instruct in order to improve the quality of learning and teaching.

IMPROVING COMMUNICATION

Effective communication is essential for success in most settings. Good communicators speak effectively and listen attentively.

Speaking

We can improve communication by:
- Stating ideas clearly
- Using common words
- Avoiding slang and words that have strong emotional meanings
- Using people's names
- Speaking in a respectful manner

Personnel Psychology

Personnel psychology is concerned with testing, selection, placement, and promotion of employees.

Job Analysis

Selecting the right person for a job, or the right job for a person, can be improved by using biographical information, interviews, and psychological tests.

Jury Selection

Who serves on a jury will affect the outcome of a trial. Psychologists often advise lawyers on which potential jurors should be selected or dismissed based on their inferred attitudes.

Environmental Problems

Environmental problems such as crowding, pollution, and wasted resources are based on human behavior. These problems can be solved only by changing behavior patterns.

Listening

Effective communication is a two-way street. We must be prepared to receive information by:
• Paying attention
• Identifying the speaker's purpose
• Waiting until they are finished to evaluate what they have said
• Watching for the information provided by nonverbal messages

CHAPTER **20** Applied Psychology

Psychology on the Web
To link to the following sites, visit *www.psychology.wadsworth.com/coon_gateways10e*

Living in Space
Articles provided by NASA about the challenges of living in space.

Mars Academy
A discussion of crew selection issues for possible trips to Mars.

Newsletter for Educational Psychologists
Recent and archived newsletters of the APA's Division 15, containing information and articles about the activities of educational psychologists.

Environmental Psychology
From the Canadian Psychological Association, this site features articles on environmental psychology, with links to other sites.

Sports Psychology
Maintained by the APA's Division 47, this site contains articles, information, and links related to exercise and sports psychology.

The Industrial-Organizational Psychologist
Online journal of the Society for Industrial-Organizational Psychology, APA Division 14.

Related Articles in InfoTrac College Edition
Go to *http://www.infotrac-college.com/wadsworth* and search by article number.

A81299951
Loughlin, C., & Barling, J. (2001, November). Young workers' work values, attitudes, and behaviours. *Journal of Occupational and Organizational Psychology, 74*(4), 543(16).

A20243402
Griffith, J. (1997, November). Student and parent perceptions of school social environment: Are they group based? *The Elementary School Journal, 98*(2), 135(16).

Interactive Learning
Links to the *PsychNow!* CD-ROM:

PsychNow! 2.0 8f. Environmental Psychology.

BEHAVIORAL STATISTICS

The results of psychological studies are often expressed as numbers, which must be summarized and interpreted before they have any meaning. Statistics bring greater clarity and precision to psychological thought and research.

Descriptive Statistics

Summarizing numbers visually, using various types of graphs, makes it easier to see trends and patterns in the results of psychological investigations.

Graphical Statistics

Graphical statistics present numbers pictorially. Different types of graphs and tables show us the data in an organized manner.

Inferential Statistics

Some statistical techniques can be used to generalize results from samples to populations, to draw conclusions, and to tell if the results of a study could have occurred by chance.

Correlation

When there is a correlation, or a consistent relationship, between scores on two measures, knowing a person's score on one measure allows us to predict his or her score on the second measure.

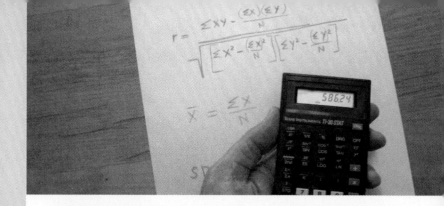

Central Tendency

We usually want to know the "average" of a group of scores, as well as how much they vary.
- The <u>mean</u> is attained by adding all the scores and dividing the total by the number of scores (the average on your exam).
- The <u>median</u> is the point at which half the scores are higher and half are lower (half of you did better and half of you did worse on the exam).

Normal Distribution

- Many psychological measures produce scores that form a normal curve (the bell curve).
- This is useful because the characteristics of normal curves are well known. From distribution curves, we can make predictions about human behavior.
- When we chart the distribution of scores, we can visualize how well they conform to the expected distribution of scores.

Appendix
Behavioral Statistics

Positive and Negative Correlations

- A <u>positive correlation</u> exists when increases in one measure are matched by increases in another measure.
- A <u>negative correlation</u> exists when an increase in one measure results in a decrease in another measure. *Note:* A "negative" correlation is not necessarily "bad." As the number of people who are inoculated against a disease increases, the number of cases of the disease decreases.

Causation vs. Correlation

Finding a correlation between two measures does not mean that one causes the other. Often two correlated measures are related due to the influence of a third variable.

Psychology on the Web
To link to the following sites, visit *www.psychology.wadsworth.com/ coon_gateways10e*

Statistics to Use
If you enter a series of numbers, this site will calculate basic descriptive statistics and more advanced inferential statistics.

Interactive Learning
Links to the PsychNow! CD-ROM:

PsychNow! 2.0 1c. Research Methods.